P9-DHM-307

To:

_____

From:

_____

Date:

_____

Message:

_____

_____

_____

The Power of a
PRAYING HUSBAND

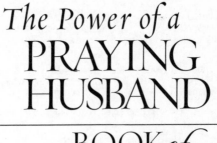

BOOK of PRAYERS

STORMIE OMARTIAN

HARVEST HOUSE PUBLISHERS

EUGENE, OREGON

Cover by Koechel Peterson & Associates, Inc., Minneapolis, Minnesota

THE POWER OF A PRAYING® HUSBAND BOOK OF PRAYERS
Copyright © 2004 by Stormie Omartian
Published by Harvest House Publishers
Eugene, Oregon 97402
www.harvesthousepublishers.com

ISBN-13: 978-0-7369-1980-7

Printed in the United States of America

09 10 11 12 13 14 /VP-KB/ 11 10 9 8 7 6 5

Covering Your
Wife in Prayer

When I wrote *The Power of a Praying® Husband*, I had many requests to have the prayers in that book made into a separate book that could be stuffed in a pocket, slipped into a briefcase, placed in a glove compartment, or propped up on a bedside table or desk. The reason being that most men lead busy lives, and even though they *want* to pray for their wives, they have trouble finding the time. And when they *do* have the time, they struggle with knowing what to pray for and how. If you are one of those men, and I suspect you are or you wouldn't be reading this, these prayers will simplify and enhance your life. Each one of the prayers will probably take less than one minute of your time to pray, but when you have prayed through all the prayers over the coming weeks, you will have covered your wife thoroughly in prayer.

I suggest that you pick a different prayer each day and as you are reminded, pray the prayer one or more times throughout the day. Tell your wife you are going to be praying for her and ask her if there is anything specific she would like you to include in your prayers.

Do not be overwhelmed by how many ways there are to pray for your wife. You don't have to do it all in a day, a week, or even a month. And it's not necessary to pray them in any particular order. Just let the Holy Spirit lead you. Refuse to worry about how and when your prayers will be answered. You don't have to make it happen. It's your job to pray. It's God's job to answer. Leave it in His hands. When you do, you will not only enjoy answers to your prayers, but you will also see great changes in yourself, your wife, and your marriage.

– Stormie Omartian –

*The effective, fervent prayer
of a righteous man avails much.*

– JAMES 5:16 –

Her Husband

*L*ord, create in *me* a clean heart and renew a right spirit within me (Psalm 51:10). Show me where my attitude and thoughts are not what You would have them to be, especially toward my wife. Convict me when I am being unforgiving. Help me to quickly let go of any anger, so that confusion will not have a place in my mind. If there is behavior in me that needs to change, enable me to make changes that last. Whatever You reveal to me, I will confess to You as sin. Make me a man after Your own heart. Enable me to be the head of my home and family just as You created me to be.

The effective, fervent prayer of
a righteous man avails much.

— JAMES 5:16 —

Prayer Notes

_____
_____
_____
_____
_____
_____
_____
_____
_____
_____
_____
_____
_____
_____
_____
_____

Her Husband

$\mathcal{L}$ord, show me how to really cover (wife's name) in prayer. Enable me to dwell with her with understanding and give honor to her so that my prayers will not be hindered (1 Peter 3:7). Renew our love for one another. Heal any wounds that have caused a rift between us. Give me patience, understanding, and compassion. Help me to be loving, tenderhearted, and courteous to her just as You ask me in Your Word (1 Peter 3:8). Enable me to love her the way that You do.

Husbands ought to love their own wives as their own bodies; he who loves his wife loves himself. For no one ever hated his own flesh, but nourishes and cherishes it, just as the Lord does the church.

— EPHESIANS 5:28-29 —

Prayer Notes

_____

_____

_____

_____

_____

_____

_____

_____

_____

_____

_____

_____

_____

Her Husband

Lord, I pray that You would bring (wife's name) and me to a new place of unity with one another. Make us be of the same mind. Show me what I need to do in order to make that come about. Give me words that heal, not wound. Fill my heart with Your love so that what overflows through my speech will be words that build up, not tear down. Convict my heart when I don't live Your way. Help me to be the man, husband, and spiritual leader that You want me to be.

*A man shall leave his father and mother
and be joined to his wife, and the two shall
become one flesh...Let each one of you in
particular so love his own wife as himself, and
let the wife see that she respects her husband.*

— EPHESIANS 5:31,33 —

Prayer Notes

_____

_____

_____

_____

_____

_____

_____

_____

_____

_____

_____

Her Spirit

Lord, I pray that You will give (wife's name) the fulfillment of knowing You in a deeper and richer way than she ever has before. Help her to be diligent and steadfast in her walk with You, never doubting or wavering. Make her strong in spirit and give her an ever-increasing faith that always believes that You will answer her prayers. Help her to carve out time every day to spend with You in Your Word and in prayer and praise. May Your words abide in her, so that when she prays You will give her the desires of her heart.

*If you abide in Me, and My words
abide in you, you will ask what you
desire, and it shall be done for you.*

– JOHN 15:7 –

Prayer Notes

_____

_____

_____

_____

_____

_____

_____

_____

_____

_____

_____

_____

_____

_____

Her Spirit

Lord, as much as I love my wife, I know You love her more. I realize that I cannot meet her every need and expectation, but You can. Help (wife's name) to increase her knowledge of You today. May she turn to You first for everything as You become her constant companion. Give her discernment and revelation and enable her to hear Your voice instructing her. Help her to stay focused on You, no matter how great the storm is around her, so that she never strays off the path You have for her. I pray You would keep me aware of when she needs a fresh filling of Your Spirit so that I will be prompted to pray for her.

Whoever drinks of the water that I shall give him will never thirst. But the water that I shall give him will become in him a fountain of water springing up into everlasting life.

– JOHN 4:14 –

Prayer Notes

_____

_____

_____

_____

_____

_____

_____

_____

_____

_____

_____

_____

_____

Her Spirit

*L*ord, help (wife's name) to be so filled with Your Spirit that people sense *Your* presence when they are in *her* presence. As Your daughter, I know she wants to serve You, but help her to understand how and when so that she may glorify You in all she does. Guide her in everything, so that she can become the dynamic, mighty woman of God You want her to be. Give her knowledge of Your will and enable her to stay in the center of it. Help her to trust You will all her heart and not depend on her own understanding. May she acknowledge You in all her ways (Proverbs 3:5-6).

The Spirit Himself bears witness with
your spirit that we are children of God.
– ROMANS 8:16 –

Prayer Notes

_____
_____
_____
_____
_____
_____
_____
_____
_____
_____
_____
_____
_____
_____
_____

Her Emotions

Lord, I am so grateful that You have made (wife's name) to be a woman of deep thoughts and feelings. I know that You have intended this for good, but I also know that the enemy of her soul will try to use it for evil. Help me to discern when he is doing that and enable me to pray accordingly. Protect her from the author of lies and help her to cast down "every high thing that exalts itself against the knowledge of God, bringing every thought into captivity to the obedience of Christ" (2 Corinthians 10:5).

Keep your heart with all diligence,
for out of it springs the issues of life.

– PROVERBS 4:23 –

Prayer Notes

Her Emotions

Lord, give (wife's name) discernment today about what she receives into her mind. I pray she will quickly identify lies about herself, her life, or her future. Help her to recognize when there is a battle going on in her mind and to be aware of the enemy's tactics. Remind her to stick to Your battle plan and rely on the sword of the Spirit, which is Your Word (Ephesians 6:17). Keep me aware of when my wife is struggling so I can talk openly with her about what is on her mind and in her heart. Enable us to communicate clearly so that we don't allow the enemy to enter in with confusion or misinterpretation.

Do not be conformed to this world, but be transformed by the renewing of your mind, that you may prove what is that good and acceptable and perfect will of God.

— ROMANS 12:2 —

Prayer Notes

_____

_____

_____

_____

_____

_____

_____

_____

_____

_____

_____

_____

Her Emotions

Lord, help me not to react inappropriately or withdraw from (wife's name) emotionally when I don't understand her. Give me patience and sensitivity, and may prayer be my *first* reaction to her emotions and not a last resort. Although I'm aware that I cannot meet my wife's every emotional need, I know that *You* can. I am not trying to absolve myself from meeting any of her needs, but I know that some of them are intended to be met only by You. I pray that You would fill her with Your peace and joy today.

The LORD redeems the soul of His
servants, and none of those who
trust in Him shall be condemned.

— PSALM 34:22 —

Prayer Notes

_____

_____

_____

_____

_____

_____

_____

_____

_____

_____

_____

_____

Her Emotions

Lord, I pray that when certain negative emotions threaten her happiness, You will be the first one (wife's name) runs to, because only You can deliver her from them. Help her to hide herself in "the secret place of Your presence" (Psalm 31:20). I pray that You would restore her soul (Psalm 23:3), heal her brokenheartedness, and bind up her wounds (Psalm 147:3). Make her to be secure in Your love and mine. Take away all fear, doubt, and discouragement, and give her clarity, joy, and peace. Help her to be quick to call on Your mighty name.

The name of the LORD is a strong tower;
the righteous run to it and are safe.

— PROVERBS 18:10 —

Prayer Notes

_____
_____
_____
_____
_____
_____
_____
_____
_____
_____
_____
_____
_____
_____
_____
_____

Her Motherhood

Lord, I pray You will help (wife's name) to be the best mother to our children (child) that she can be. Give her strength, and help her to understand that she can do all things through Christ who strengthens her (Philippians 4:13). Give her patience, kindness, gentleness, and discernment. Guard her tongue so that the words she speaks will build up and not tear down, will bring life and not destruction. Guide her as she makes decisions regarding each child. I also bring before You my own concerns about (name any area of concern that you have for that child). I trust that You will help us be the best parents we can be.

Her children rise up and call her blessed;
her husband also, and he praises her.

— PROVERBS 31:28 —

Prayer Notes

_____

_____

_____

_____

_____

_____

_____

_____

_____

_____

_____

_____

_____

Her Motherhood

*L*ord, I know that (wife's name) and I cannot successfully raise our children without You. So I ask that You would take the burden of raising them from our shoulders and partner with us to bring them up. Give (wife's name) and me patience, strength, and wisdom to train, teach, discipline, and care for each child. Help us to understand each child's needs and know how to meet them. Give us discernment about what we allow into the home through TV, books, movies, video games, magazines, and computer activities. Give us revelation and the ability each day to see what we need to see.

*Pour out your heart like water before the
face of the LORD. Lift your hands toward
Him for the life of your young children.*

— LAMENTATIONS 2:19 —

Prayer Notes

_____

_____

_____

_____

_____

_____

_____

_____

_____

_____

_____

_____

_____

_____

Her Motherhood

Lord, show (wife's name) and me Your perspective on each of our children's uniqueness and potential for greatness. Give us a balance between being overprotective and allowing our children to experience life too early. I ask You for the gifts of intelligence, strength, talent, wisdom, and godliness to be in our children. Keep them safe from any accident, disease, or evil influence. May no plan of the enemy succeed in their lives. Help (wife's name) and me to raise our children (child) to be obedient and respectful to both of us and to have a heart to follow You and Your Word. I pray that my wife will find fulfillment, contentment, and joy as a mother, while never losing sight of who she is in You.

*They shall not labor in vain, nor bring
forth children for trouble; for they shall
be the descendants of the blessed of the
L*ORD*, and their offspring with them.*

– ISAIAH 65:23 –

Prayer Notes

_____

_____

_____

_____

_____

_____

_____

_____

_____

_____

_____

_____

Her Moods

Lord, I pray for (wife's name) and ask that You would calm her spirit, soothe her soul, and give her peace today. Drown out the voice of the enemy, who seeks to entrap her with lies. Help her to take every thought captive so she is not led astray (2 Corinthians 10:5). Where there is error in her thinking, I pray You would reveal it to her and set her back on course. Help her to hear Your voice only. Fill her afresh with Your Holy Spirit and wash away anything in her that is not of You.

I will hear what God the LORD *will speak, for He will speak peace to His people and to His saints...*

— PSALM 85:8 —

Prayer Notes

_____

_____

_____

_____

_____

_____

_____

_____

_____

_____

_____

_____

_____

_____

Her Moods

Lord, I pray that You would balance my wife's body perfectly today so that she is not emotionally carried up and down like a roller coaster. Give (wife's name) inner tranquility that prevails no matter what is going on around her. Enable her to see things from Your perspective so that she can fully appreciate all the good that is in her life. Keep her from being blinded by fear and doubt. Show her the bigger picture, and teach her to distinguish the valuable from the unimportant.

You will keep him in perfect peace, whose
mind is stayed on You, because he trusts in You.
— ISAIAH 26:3 —

Prayer Notes

_____

_____

_____

_____

_____

_____

_____

_____

_____

_____

_____

_____

_____

Her Moods

Lord, help (wife's name) to recognize the answers to her own prayers. Show me how to convince her that I love her, and help me to be able to demonstrate it in ways she can perceive. I know that You have "called us to peace" (1 Corinthians 7:15). Help us both to hear that call and live in the peace that passes all understanding. I say to my wife, "Let the peace of God rule" in your heart, and "be thankful" (Colossians 3:15).

*The peace of God, which surpasses all
understanding, will guard your hearts
and minds through Christ Jesus.*

– PHILIPPIANS 4:7 –

Prayer Notes

_____
_____
_____
_____
_____
_____
_____
_____
_____
_____
_____
_____
_____
_____

Her Marriage

Lord, I pray that You would establish in me and (wife's name) bonds of love that cannot be broken. Show me how to love my wife in an ever-deepening way that she can clearly recognize. May we have mutual respect and admiration for each other so that we become and remain one another's greatest friend, champion, and unwavering support. Where love has been diminished, lost, destroyed, or buried under hurt and disappointment, put it back in our hearts. Give us strength to hold on to the good in our marriage, even in those times when one of us doesn't *feel* love.

This is My commandment, that you
love one another as I have loved you.
– JOHN 15:12 –

Prayer Notes

_____

_____

_____

_____

_____

_____

_____

_____

_____

_____

_____

_____

_____

_____

Her Marriage

*L*ord, enable (wife's name) and me to forgive each other quickly and completely. Specifically I lift up to You (name any area where forgiveness is needed). Help us to "be kind to one another, tenderhearted, forgiving," the way You are to us (Ephesians 4:32). Give us a sense of humor, especially as we deal with the hard issues of life. Unite us in faith, beliefs, standards of morality, and mutual trust. Help us to be of the same mind, to move together in harmony, and to quickly come to mutual agreements about our finances, our children, how we spend our time, and any other decisions that need to be made.

*Therefore, as the elect of God, holy and
beloved, put on tender mercies, kindness,
humility, meekness, longsuffering; bearing
with one another, and forgiving one another...*

– COLOSSIANS 3:12-13 –

Prayer Notes

_____

_____

_____

_____

_____

_____

_____

_____

_____

_____

_____

_____

_____

Her Marriage

Lord, where (wife's name) and I are in disagreement and this has caused strife, I pray You would draw us together on the issues. Adjust our perspectives to align with Yours. Make our communication open and honest so that we avoid misunderstandings. May we have the grace to be tolerant of each other's faults and, at the same time, have the willingness to change. I pray that we will not live two separate lives, but will instead walk together as a team. Remind us to take time for one another so that our marriage will be a source of happiness, peace, and joy for us both.

Behold, how good and how pleasant it
is for brethren to dwell together in unity!
— PSALM 133:1 —

Prayer Notes

_____
_____
_____
_____
_____
_____
_____
_____
_____
_____
_____
_____
_____
_____
_____
_____

Her Marriage

Lord, I pray that You would protect our marriage from anything that would destroy it. Take out of our lives anyone who would come between us or tempt us. Help (wife's name) and me to immediately recognize and resist temptation when it presents itself. I pray that no other relationship either of us have, or have had in the past, will rob us of anything in our relationship now. Sever all unholy ties in both of our lives. May there never be any adultery or divorce in our future to destroy what You, Lord, have put together.

But the Lord is faithful, who will
establish you and guard you from the evil one.
— 2 THESSALONIANS 3:3 —

Prayer Notes

_____
_____
_____
_____
_____
_____
_____
_____
_____
_____
_____
_____
_____
_____
_____
_____
_____

Her Submission

Lord, I submit myself to You this day. Lead me as I lead my family. Help me to make all decisions based on Your revelation and guidance. As I submit my leadership to You, enable (wife's name) to fully trust that You are leading me. Help her to understand the kind of submission You want from her. Help me to understand the kind of submission You want from me. Enable me to be the leader You want me to be. I pray that I will allow You, Lord, to be so in control of my life that my wife will be able to freely trust Your Holy Spirit working in me.

Wives, submit to your own husbands,
as to the Lord. For the husband is head
of the wife, as also Christ is head of the
church; and He is the Savior of the body.

— EPHESIANS 5:22, 23 —

Prayer Notes

Her Submission

Lord, where (wife's name) and I disagree on certain issues, help us to settle them in proper order. Help me to love my wife the way You love me, so that I will gain her complete respect and love. Give her a submissive heart and the faith she needs to trust me to be the spiritual leader in our home. At the same time, help both of us to submit "to one another in the fear of God" (Ephesians 5:21). I know that only You, Lord, can make that perfect balance happen in our lives.

*Husbands, love your wives, just as Christ also
loved the church and gave Himself for her...*
— EPHESIANS 5:25 —

Prayer Notes

_____

_____

_____

_____

_____

_____

_____

_____

_____

_____

_____

_____

_____

_____

Her Relationships

Lord, I pray for (wife's name) to have good, strong, healthy relationships with godly women. May each of these women add strength to her life and be a strong prayer support for her. I also pray for good relationships with all family members. May Your spirit of love and acceptance reign in each one. I pray for a resolution of any uncomfortable in-law relationships for either of us. Show me what I can do or say to make a positive difference. Specifically I pray for my wife's relationship with (name of friend or family member). Bring reconciliation and restoration where that relationship has broken down.

The righteous should choose his friends carefully,
for the way of the wicked leads them astray.

— PROVERBS 12:26 —

Prayer Notes

_____

_____

_____

_____

_____

_____

_____

_____

_____

_____

_____

_____

_____

_____

Her Relationships

Lord, I pray that (wife's name) will be a forgiving person. Show her that forgiveness doesn't make the other person right, it makes *her free*. If she has any unforgiveness she is unaware of, reveal it to her so she can confess it before You and be released from it. I especially pray that there would be no unforgiveness between us. Enable us to forgive one another quickly and completely. Remind us often that You, Lord, are the only One who knows the whole story, so we don't have the right to judge. Make my wife a light to her family, friends, co-workers, and community, and may all her relationships be glorifying to You, Lord.

Whenever you stand praying, if you have anything against anyone, forgive him, that your Father in heaven may also forgive you your trespasses.

— MARK 11:25 —

Prayer Notes

_____

_____

_____

_____

_____

_____

_____

_____

_____

_____

_____

_____

_____

Her Priorities

Lord, show (wife's name) how to seek You first in all things, and to make time with You her first priority every day. Give her the wisdom to know how to effectively divide up her time, and then to make the best use of it. Show her the way to prioritize her responsibilities and interests and still fulfill each role she has to the fullest. Show her how to find a good balance between being a wife, taking care of children and others, running a home, doing her work, serving in the church and community, and finding time for herself so that she can be rested and refreshed.

To everything there is a season, a
time for every purpose under heaven.
— ECCLESIASTES 3:1 —

Prayer Notes

_____
_____
_____
_____
_____
_____
_____
_____
_____
_____
_____
_____
_____
_____
_____

Her Priorities

*L*ord, release (wife's name) from the guilt that can weigh her down when things get out of balance. In the midst of all that she does, I pray that she will take time for me without feeling she is neglecting other things. Give her the energy and the ability to accomplish all she needs to do, and may she have joy in the process. Give (wife's name) the grace to handle the challenges she faces each day, and the wisdom to not try to do more than she can. Teach her to clearly recognize what her priorities should be, and enable her to balance them well.

*Seek first the kingdom of God
and His righteousness, and all
these things shall be added to you.*

– MATTHEW 6:33 –

Prayer Notes

_____

_____

_____

_____

_____

_____

_____

_____

_____

_____

_____

_____

_____

_____

Her Priorities

*L*ord, help (wife's name) to make our home a peaceful sanctuary. Regardless of our financial state, give her the wisdom, energy, strength, vision, and clarity of mind to transform our dwelling into a beautiful place of refuge that brings joy to each of us. Show me how I can encourage and assist her in that. Holy Spirit, I invite You to fill our home with Your peace, truth, love, and unity. Through wisdom let our house be built, and by understanding may it be established. Reveal to us anything that is in our house that is not glorifying to You, Lord. I say that "as for me and my house, we will serve the LORD" (Joshua 24:15).

She watches over the ways of her household,
and does not eat the bread of idleness.

— PROVERBS 31:27 —

Prayer Notes

_____

_____

_____

_____

_____

_____

_____

_____

_____

_____

_____

_____

_____

_____

Her Beauty

$\mathcal{L}$ord, I pray that You would give (wife's name) the "incorruptible beauty of a gentle and quiet spirit, which is very precious" in Your sight (1 Peter 3:4). Help her to appreciate the beauty You have put in her. Make my wife beautiful in every way, and may everyone else see the beauty of Your image reflected in her, but remind her that time spent in Your presence is the best beauty treatment of all. Help me to remember to encourage her and speak words that will make her feel beautiful.

*One thing I have desired of the LORD, that
will I seek: that I may dwell in the house of the
LORD all the days of my life, to behold the beauty
of the LORD, and to inquire in His temple.*

– PSALM 27:4 –

Prayer Notes

_____

_____

_____

_____

_____

_____

_____

_____

_____

_____

_____

_____

Her Beauty

Lord, where anyone in the past has convinced (wife's name) that she is unattractive and less than who You made her to be, I pray that You would replace those lies with Your truth. I pray that she will not base her worth on appearance, but on Your Word. Convince her of how valuable she is to You, so that I will be better able to convince her of how valuable she is to me. Show my wife how to take good care of herself. Give her wisdom about the way she dresses and adorns herself so that it always enhances her beauty to the fullest and glorifies You.

The King will greatly desire your beauty;
because He is your LORD, worship Him.

— PSALM 45:11 —

Prayer Notes

_____

_____

_____

_____

_____

_____

_____

_____

_____

_____

_____

_____

_____

_____

Her Sexuality

Lord, I pray that You would bless (wife's name) today, and especially bless our marriage and our sexual relationship. Help me to be unselfish and understanding toward her. Help her to be unselfish and understanding toward me. Teach us to show affection to one another in ways that keep romance and desire alive between us. Where one of us is more affectionate than the other, balance that out. Help us to remember to touch each other in an affectionate way every day. I pray that how often we come together sexually will be agreeable to both of us.

*Let each man have his own wife, and let each
woman have her own husband. Let the
husband render to his wife the affection due
her, and likewise also the wife to her husband.*

– 1 Corinthians 7:2-3 –

Prayer Notes

_____

_____

_____

_____

_____

_____

_____

_____

_____

_____

_____

Her Sexuality

Lord, show me if I ever hurt (wife's name), and help me to apologize in a way that will cause her to forgive me completely. Any time we have an argument or a breakdown of communication, enable us to get over it quickly and come back together physically so no room is made for the devil to work. If ever the fire between us dies into a suffocating smoke, I pray that You would clear the air and rekindle the flame.

*Marriage is honorable among
all, and the bed undefiled.*

— HEBREWS 13:4 —

Prayer Notes

_____
_____
_____
_____
_____
_____
_____
_____
_____
_____
_____
_____
_____
_____

Her Sexuality

Lord, help me to always treat (wife's name) with respect and honor and never say anything that would demean her, even in jest. Help me to be considerate of her when she is exhausted or not feeling well. But I also pray that she would understand my sexual needs and be considerate of those as well. Only You can help us find that balance. Make our sexual relationship fulfilling, enjoyable, freeing, and refreshing for both of us. May our intimacy bond the two of us together and connect our hearts and emotions as well as our bodies. Help us to freely communicate our needs and desires to one another.

The wife does not have authority over her own body, but the husband does. And likewise the husband does not have authority over his own body, but the wife does.

– 1 Corinthians 7:4 –

Prayer Notes

_____

_____

_____

_____

_____

_____

_____

_____

_____

_____

_____

_____

_____

_____

Her Sexuality

Lord, keep my wife's heart and my heart always faithful. Take out of our lives anyone or anything that would cause temptation. Where there has been unfaithfulness in thought or deed on the part of either of us, I pray for full repentance, cleansing, and release from it. Keep us free from anything that would cause us to neglect this vital area of our lives. May our desire always be only for each other. Renew and revitalize our sexual relationship, and make it all You created it to be.

Therefore what God has joined
together, let no man separate.
– MARK 10:9 –

Prayer Notes

_____
_____
_____
_____
_____
_____
_____
_____
_____
_____
_____
_____
_____
_____

Her Fears

*L*ord, I pray that You would help (wife's name) to "be anxious for nothing" (Philippians 4:6).

Remind her to bring all her concerns to You in prayer so that Your peace that passes all understanding will permanently reside in her heart. Specifically I pray about (anything that causes your wife to have fear). I ask You to set her free from that fear and comfort her this day. I stand against any enemy attacks targeted at my wife, and I say that a spirit of fear will have no place in her life. Strengthen her faith in You, Lord, to be her Defender.

I sought the LORD, and He heard me,
and delivered me from all my fears.

— PSALM 34:4 —

Prayer Notes

_____

_____

_____

_____

_____

_____

_____

_____

_____

_____

_____

_____

_____

_____

Her Fears

Lord, enable (wife's name) to rise above the criticism of others and be delivered from fear of their opinions. May her only concern be with pleasing you. I say to my wife, "Be strong in the Lord and in the power of His might" (Ephesians 6:10). "In righteousness you shall be established; you shall be far from oppression, for you shall not fear; and from terror, for it shall not come near you" (Isaiah 54:14). Enable my wife to rise up and say, "The LORD is my light and my salvation; whom shall I fear? The LORD is the strength of my life; of whom shall I be afraid?" (Psalm 27:1).

The fear of man brings a snare, but whoever trusts in the LORD shall be safe.

— PROVERBS 29:25 —

Prayer Notes

_____

_____

_____

_____

_____

_____

_____

_____

_____

_____

_____

_____

_____

_____

Her Fears

Lord, give (wife's name) strength in the tough times of her life. Sustain her with Your presence so that nothing will shake her. Enable her to rise above the things that challenge her. Specifically I lift up to You (your wife's greatest need, weakness, struggle, or temptation). Help her separate herself from that which tempts her. I say to (wife's name) that "no temptation has overtaken you except such as is common to man; but God is faithful, who will not allow you to be tempted beyond what you are able, but with the temptation will also make the way of escape, that you may be able to bear it" (1 Corinthians 10:13).

God has not given us a spirit of fear, but of power and of love and of a sound mind.
— 2 TIMOTHY 1:7 —

Prayer Notes

_____

_____

_____

_____

_____

_____

_____

_____

_____

_____

_____

_____

_____

Her Fears

Lord, give (wife's name) patience while she is waiting for her prayers to be answered and for all things to be accomplished. Help her to wait upon You instead of waiting for things to change. Cause her to fear only You and to be content where she is this moment, knowing that You will not leave her there forever. Perfect her in Your "perfect love" that "casts out fear," so that fear has no room in her soul (1 John 4:18). Remind her to "wait on the LORD; be of good courage, and He shall strengthen your heart" (Psalm 27:14).

*I wait for the LORD, my soul
waits, and in His word I do hope.*

— PSALM 130:5 —

Prayer Notes

_____
_____
_____
_____
_____
_____
_____
_____
_____
_____
_____
_____
_____
_____

Her Purpose

Lord, I know that You have placed within (wife's name) special gifts and talents that are to be used for Your purpose and Your glory. Show her what they are, and show me too, Lord, that I may encourage her. Help her to know that You have something in particular for her to do and have given her a ministry that only she can fulfill. Give her a sense of Your call on her life, and open doors of opportunity for her to develop and use her gifts in that calling. Bring her into alignment with Your ultimate purpose for her life, and may she be fulfilled in it.

In Him also we have obtained an inheritance,
being predestined according to the purpose of
Him who works all things according to the
counsel of His will, that we who first trusted
in Christ should be to the praise of His glory.

— EPHESIANS 1:11-12 —

Prayer Notes

_____

_____

_____

_____

_____

_____

_____

_____

_____

_____

_____

_____

Her Purpose

Lord, I pray that (wife's name) will be the wife You have called her to be and the wife I need her to be. What I need most from my wife right now is (name the need most pressing on your heart). Show me what my wife needs from me. Help us to fulfill one another in these areas without requiring of each other more than we can be. Keep us from having unrealistic expectations of each other when our expectations should be in You. Help us to recognize the gifts You have placed in each of us and to encourage one another in their development and nurture.

Having then gifts differing according to the
grace that is given to us, let us use them...
– ROMANS 12:6 –

Prayer Notes

_____

_____

_____

_____

_____

_____

_____

_____

_____

_____

_____

_____

_____

_____

Her Purpose

Thank You, Lord, for the wife You have given me (Proverbs 19:14). Release her into Your perfect plan for her life so that she will fulfill the destiny You've given her. Use her gifts and talents to bless others. I say to (wife's name), you are "like a fruitful vine in the very heart of your house" (Psalm 128:3). "Many daughters have done well, but you excel them all" (Proverbs 31:29). "Let your light so shine before men, that they may see your good works and glorify your Father in heaven" (Matthew 5:16). Lord, grant my wife according to her heart's desire, and fulfill all her purpose (Psalm 20:4).

[It is God] who has saved us and called us with a holy calling, not according to our works, but according to His own purpose and grace which was given to us in Christ Jesus before time began.

– 2 Timothy 1:9 –

Prayer Notes

_____

_____

_____

_____

_____

_____

_____

_____

_____

_____

_____

_____

Her Trust

Lord, I pray that You would give (wife's name) the ability to trust me in all things. Most of all, I want her to trust Your Holy Spirit working in me and through me. Where I have not been worthy of that trust, show me, and I will confess that before You as sin. Help me not to conduct myself that way anymore. Make me always be worthy of her trust. Show me how to convince her that I am in partnership with You and will do all I can to be trustworthy. Increase our faith, for I know that You are a shield to those who put their trust in You (Proverbs 30:5).

As for God, His way is perfect; the word of the LORD is proven; He is a shield to all who trust in Him.

– 2 SAMUEL 22:31 –

Prayer Notes

_____

_____

_____

_____

_____

_____

_____

_____

_____

_____

_____

_____

Her Trust

Lord, where (wife's name) has lost trust in me unjustly, I pray You would help her to see the truth. If she doesn't trust me because of something someone else has done to her, help her to forgive that person so she can be free. I pray that she will not project those failures onto me and expect that I will do the same thing. Specifically I pray about (name any area where there is a lack of trust). Wherever we have broken trust with one another, help us to reestablish it and make it strong. May we both trust You, Lord, working in each of us.

Let him trust in the name of the
LORD and rely upon his God.

– ISAIAH 50:10 –

Prayer Notes

_____
_____
_____
_____
_____
_____
_____
_____
_____
_____
_____
_____
_____
_____

Her Trust

Lord, break any unholy bonds or soul ties between me and any other woman in my past. Break any unholy bonds or soul ties between my wife and any other man in her past. Help us to fully repent of all relationships outside of our own that were not glorifying to You. Lord, I pray that You would deepen my trust of my wife. Show me if there are places where I don't trust her judgment, her abilities, her loyalty, or her decisions. I pray that she will always be a trustworthy person and that I will be able to trust her completely.

*Cause me to hear Your lovingkindness in
the morning, for in You do I trust;
cause me to know the way in which I
should walk, for I lift up my soul to You.*

— PSALM 143:8 —

Prayer Notes

_____
_____
_____
_____
_____
_____
_____
_____
_____
_____
_____
_____
_____
_____

Her Protection

Lord, I pray that You would surround (wife's name) with Your hand of protection. Keep her safe from any accidents, diseases, or evil influences. Protect her in cars, planes, or wherever she is. Keep her out of harm's way. Let no weapon formed against my wife be able to prosper (Isaiah 54:17). Shield her from the plans of evil people. Thank You, Lord, that this day You will cover (wife's name) and will help her to lie down in peace, and sleep; for You alone, O Lord, make her to dwell in safety (Psalm 4:8).

The LORD is my rock and my fortress and my deliverer; my God, my strength, in whom I will trust; my shield and the horn of my salvation, my stronghold. I will call upon the LORD, who is worthy to be praised; so shall I be saved from my enemies.

– PSALM 18:2-3 –

Prayer Notes

_____

_____

_____

_____

_____

_____

_____

_____

_____

_____

_____

Her Protection

Lord, I pray that You would help (wife's name) to truly see that her body is Your dwelling place. Enable her to protect her body through right choices in what she eats. Give her the motivation to exercise regularly so that she has endurance. Help her to get plenty of rest so that she is completely rejuvenated when she awakens. May she acknowledge You in all her ways—including the care of her body—so that You can direct her paths. Watch over her as she moves through her day and performs the tasks that demand her time and attention.

*You were bought at a price; therefore glorify God
in your body and in your spirit, which are God's.*

– 1 CORINTHIANS 6:20 –

Prayer Notes

_____

_____

_____

_____

_____

_____

_____

_____

_____

_____

_____

_____

_____

Her Protection

Lord, give Your angels charge over (wife's name) to keep her in all her ways (Psalm 91:11). I say to my wife that God will "cover you with His feathers, and under His wings you shall take refuge; His truth shall be your shield and buckler. You shall not be afraid of the terror by night, nor of the arrow that flies by day, nor of the pestilence that walks in darkness, nor of the destruction that lays waste at noonday. A thousand may fall at your side, and ten thousand at your right hand; but it shall not come near you" (Psalm 91:4-7).

The angel of the LORD encamps all around
those who fear Him, and delivers them.

– PSALM 34:7 –

Prayer Notes

_____

_____

_____

_____

_____

_____

_____

_____

_____

_____

_____

_____

_____

_____

Her Desires

Lord, I pray that You would touch (wife's name) this day and fulfill her deepest desires. In the midst of all she has to do, let there be ample time for what she enjoys most. Help her to surrender her dreams to You so that You can bring to life the ones You have placed in her heart. I pray that she will never try to follow a dream of her own making, one that You will not bless. Help her to surrender *her* plans so that You can reveal *Your* plan. I know that in Your plan, timing is everything. May she reach for her highest dreams in Your perfect timing.

He will fulfill the desire of those who fear Him;
He also will hear their cry and save them.

– PSALM 145:19 –

Prayer Notes

_____

_____

_____

_____

_____

_____

_____

_____

_____

_____

_____

_____

_____

Her Desires

Lord, help me understand the things that interest (wife's name). I also pray that You would make a way for us to share (name a specific activity or interest you would like to do together). Help her to understand my enjoyment of it, and may she develop an appreciation for it too. I know that You would not give us dreams that aren't compatible. I pray that the desires of our hearts will be perfectly knitted together. May we not only be caught up in our own dreams but in each other's as well. Help us to always share with one another the deepest desires of our hearts.

You open Your hand and satisfy
the desire of every living thing.

— PSALM 145:16 —

Prayer Notes

_____
_____
_____
_____
_____
_____
_____
_____
_____
_____
_____
_____
_____
_____
_____
_____

Her Work

Lord, I pray that You would help (wife's name) to be successful in her work. No matter what her work is at any given time, establish it and help her to find favor through it. Thank You for the abilities, gifts, and creativity You have placed in her. Continue to reveal, develop, and refine those gifts and talents, and use them for Your purposes. May her skills increase in value, and may she excel in each of them. Open doors for her that no man can shut, and bless her with success. Give her the gift of work that she loves and establish the work of her hands (Psalm 90:17).

The labor of the righteous leads to life.

— PROVERBS 10:16 —

Prayer Notes

_____

_____

_____

_____

_____

_____

_____

_____

_____

_____

_____

_____

_____

_____

Her Work

*L*ord, I pray that You would keep my wife and me from ever being in competition with one another, and help us to always rejoice in each other's accomplishments. Help us to build one another up and not forget that we are on the same team. Show me how I can encourage (wife's name). Lord, Your Word says when we commit our work to You, the financial blessing we receive will not bring misery along with it (Proverbs 10:22). You have also said "the laborer is worthy of his wages" (1 Timothy 5:18). I pray that (wife's name) will be rewarded well for her labor and that it will bless her, our family, and others.

Give her of the fruit of her hands, and
let her own works praise her in the gates.

– PROVERBS 31:31 –

Prayer Notes

_____
_____
_____
_____
_____
_____
_____
_____
_____
_____
_____
_____
_____
_____
_____

Her Deliverance

Lord, I pray that You would set (wife's name) free from anything that holds her other than You. Deliver her from any memory of the past that has the power to control her or keep her trapped in its grip. Help her to forgive any person who has hurt her so that unforgiveness will not be able to hold her captive. Set her free from everything that keeps her from being all You created her to be. Keep her protected from the plans of the enemy so that he cannot thwart the deliverance and healing You want to bring about in her life.

Do not remember the former things, nor consider the things of old. Behold, I will do a new thing, now it shall spring forth; shall you not know it? I will even make a road in the wilderness and rivers in the desert.

– ISAIAH 43:18-19 –

Prayer Notes

_____

_____

_____

_____

_____

_____

_____

_____

_____

_____

_____

_____

Her Deliverance

Lord, I ask that You would restore all that has ever been stolen from (wife's name) until she is lacking no good thing. I know that in Your presence is healing and wholeness. Help (wife's name) to live in Your presence so that she can be made totally whole. I know that "though we walk in the flesh, we do not war according to the flesh. For the weapons of our warfare are not carnal but mighty in God for pulling down strongholds" (2 Corinthians 10:3-4). In the name of Jesus I pull down any strongholds the enemy has erected around (wife's name).

*The Lord will deliver me from every evil
work and preserve me for His heavenly
kingdom. To Him be glory forever and ever.*

– 2 TIMOTHY 4:18 –

Prayer Notes

_____

_____

_____

_____

_____

_____

_____

_____

_____

_____

_____

_____

_____

Her Deliverance

Lord, today I pray that (wife's name) will find freedom from (name a specific area of struggle from which your wife needs to find freedom). Set her free from this in the name of Jesus. I pray that for her sake You "will not rest, until her righteousness goes forth as brightness, and her salvation as a lamp that burns" (Isaiah 62:1). Make darkness light before her "and crooked places straight" (Isaiah 42:16). You have said in Your Word that "whoever walks wisely will be delivered" (Proverbs 28:26). I pray she will walk with wisdom and find full deliverance. Show me how to love and support her well in the process.

*If anyone is in Christ, he is a new
creation; old things have passed away;
behold, all things have become new.*

– 2 Corinthians 5:17 –

Prayer Notes

_____
_____
_____
_____
_____
_____
_____
_____
_____
_____
_____
_____
_____
_____
_____

Her Obedience

Lord, I pray that You would enable (wife's name) to live in total obedience to Your laws and Your ways. Help her to see where her thoughts and actions are not lined up with Your directions as to how she is to live. Keep my wife from doing anything that separates her from the fullness of Your presence and Your love. Help her to hear Your instructions, and give her the desire to do what You ask. Remind her to confess any error quickly, and enable her to take the steps of obedience she needs to take. Show her where she is not living in obedience, and help her to do what she needs to do.

If they obey and serve Him, they shall spend their days in prosperity, and their years in pleasures.

— JOB 36:11 —

Prayer Notes

_____

_____

_____

_____

_____

_____

_____

_____

_____

_____

_____

_____

_____

_____

Her Obedience

Lord, Your Word says, "He who obeys instruction guards his life" (Proverbs 19:16 NIV). Bless my wife's mind, emotions, and will as she takes steps of obedience. Your Word also says that "out of the overflow of the heart the mouth speaks" (Matthew 12:34 NIV). Fill my wife's heart with Your love, peace, and joy this day so that the sweetness of Your presence within her overflows in her words. May Your Spirit control her tongue so that everything she speaks brings life. Help (wife's name) to say as David did, "I have resolved that my mouth will not sin" (Psalm 17:3 NIV).

*Do not forget my law, but let your heart
keep my commands; for length of days and
long life and peace they will add to you.*
— PROVERBS 3:1-2 —

Prayer Notes

_____
_____
_____
_____
_____
_____
_____
_____
_____
_____
_____
_____
_____

Her Obedience

*L*ord, Your Word says, "No good thing will He withhold from those who walk uprightly" (Psalm 84:11). I pray that (wife's name) will walk uprightly and that You will pour out Your blessings upon her. Especially bless her with the peace and long life You speak of in Your Word (Proverbs 3:1-2). I pray this day that my wife will walk in obedience to You and that You will reward her with an abundance of good things. Let the words of her mouth and the meditation of her heart be always acceptable in Your sight, O Lord, our strength and our Redeemer (Psalm 19:14).

The path of the just is like the shining sun,
that shines ever brighter unto the perfect day.

— PROVERBS 4:18 —

Prayer Notes

_____

_____

_____

_____

_____

_____

_____

_____

_____

_____

_____

_____

_____

_____

Her Future

Lord, I pray for (wife's name) to have total peace about the past, present, and future of her life. Give her a vision for her future that makes her certain she is safe in Your hands. Free her completely from the past so that nothing interferes with the future You have for her. Help her to see her future from Your perspective and not believe any lies of the enemy about it. May she trust Your promise that the plans You have for her are for good and not evil, to give her a future and a hope (Jeremiah 29:11 NIV).

*Eye has not seen, nor ear heard, nor have
entered into the heart of man the things which
God has prepared for those who love Him.*

— 1 CORINTHIANS 2:9 —

Prayer Notes

_____

_____

_____

_____

_____

_____

_____

_____

_____

_____

_____

_____

Her Future

Lord, I pray that You would give (wife's name) wisdom in all things now and in the days to come. Give her confidence that the future is something she never has to fear. Give her wisdom in her work, travels, relationships, and finances. Bless her with the discernment to distinguish the truth from a lie. May she have the contentment, longevity, enjoyment, vitality, riches, and happiness that Your Word says are there for those who find wisdom (Proverbs 3:16-18). May she also find protection, grace, rest, freedom from fear, and confidence in You (Proverbs 3:21-26).

There is surely a future hope for you,
and your hope will not be cut off.

— Proverbs 23:18 (NIV) —

Prayer Notes

_____

_____

_____

_____

_____

_____

_____

_____

_____

_____

_____

_____

_____

_____

Her Future

Lord, I ask that You would take (wife's name) from glory to glory and strength to strength as she learns to depend on Your wisdom and not lean on her own understanding. When she needs to make any decision, I pray that You, Holy Spirit, will guide her. For the decisions we make together, give us wisdom to make them in unity. Specifically I pray for (name a decision you must make together). Help us to know Your will in this matter. I pray that we will make godly choices and decisions that are pleasing to You.

When He, the Spirit of truth, has
come, He will guide you into all truth.
– JOHN 16:13 –

Prayer Notes

_____
_____
_____
_____
_____
_____
_____
_____
_____
_____
_____
_____
_____
_____

Her Future

Lord, I pray that (wife's name) will be planted in Your house and flourish in Your courts. May the fruit of her life be seen every year, and even into old age may she be fresh and flourishing (Psalm 92:13-14). Bless her with long life, and when she comes to the end of her life, may it not be one moment before Your chosen time. Let that transition also be attended with peace and joy, and the absence of suffering. Let it be said of her that she was Your light to the world around her.

*For I know the thoughts I think toward
you, says the LORD, thoughts of peace and
not of evil, to give you a future and a hope.*

— JEREMIAH 29:11 —

Prayer Notes

_____

_____

_____

_____

_____

_____

_____

_____

_____

_____

_____

_____

_____

OTHER BOOKS
by STORMIE OMARTIAN

The Power of a Praying® Woman
Stormie Omartian's bestselling books have helped hundreds of thousands of individuals pray more effectively for their spouses, their children, and their nation. Now she has written a book on a subject she knows intimately: being a praying woman. Stormie's deep knowledge of Scripture and candid examples from her own prayer life provide guidance for women who seek to trust God with deep longings and cover every area of life with prayer.

The Power of a Praying® Wife
Stormie shares how wives can develop a deeper relationship with their husbands by praying for them. With this practical advice on praying for specific areas, including decision-making, fears, spiritual strength, and sexuality, women will discover the fulfilling marriage God intended.

The Power of a Praying® Husband
Building on the success of *The Power of a Praying® Wife*, Stormie offers this guide to help husbands pray more effectively for their wives. Each chapter features comments from well-known Christian men, biblical wisdom, and prayer ideas.

The Power of a Praying® Parent
This powerful book for parents offers 30 easy-to-read chapters that focus on specific areas of prayers for children. This personal, practical guide leads the way to enriched, strong prayer lives for both moms and dads.

Just Enough Light for the Step I'm On
New Christians and those experiencing life changes or difficult times will appreciate Stormie's honesty, candor, and advice based on experience and the Word of God in this collection of devotional readings perfect for the pressures of today's world.